# There's a Bug on My Book!

### Written and Illustrated by
## John Himmelman

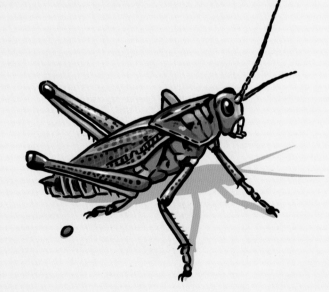

Dawn Publications

# For the kids at Platt Nature Center, who LOVE bugs on their books!

**Library of Congress Cataloging-in-Publication Data**
Names: Himmelman, John, author illustrator.
Title: There's a bug on my book! / written and illustrated by John Himmelman.
Description: First edition. | Nevada City, CA : Dawn Publications, [2017]
Identifiers: LCCN 2016024977| ISBN 9781584695875 (hard)
| ISBN 9781584695882  (pbk.)
Subjects:  LCSH: Insects--Juvenile literature.
Classification: LCC QL467.2 .H555 2017 | DDC 595.7--dc23
LC record available at https://lccn.loc.gov/2016024977

Book design and computer production by Patty Arnold, *Menagerie Design & Publishing*
Manufactured by Regent Publishing Services, Hong Kong
Printed December, 2016, in ShenZhen, Guangdong, China
10 9 8 7 6 5 4 3 2 1
First Edition

**Dawn Publications**
12402 Bitney Springs Road
Nevada City, CA 95959
530-274-7775
nature@dawnpub.com

Let's read outside in the fresh air and sunshine!
We'll lay the book right here
on the grass.

Hey, there's a bug on my book!
It's a beetle.

Move it along with a puff of breath.

It opens its wings and takes off with a buzz.

Beetles fly.

**Wow,** a snake!

Slithering right across the page! Looking for a tasty beetle?

*Tilt the book* so the snake can slide into the grass. Then lay it back down.

Oh, it's coiling itself around the page!
And it looks like it may stay a while.

Snakes coil.

Whoa! A grasshopper just landed!

Let's give it a nudge
to move it along.

It's gone in a blink.

Grasshoppers hop.

A spider! It must have fallen
from the tree above.

Pick the book up and
**tip the *top*** of the book
toward you until the spider
hangs down.

The spider rides a string of silk to the ground.

Spiders hang

Lay the book back down.

## Now what?

A worm just crawled up from the ground.
It probably doesn't want to be here.

Let's push it off.
No squishing.

Twitch and squirm. Off the page it goes.

Worms wiggle.

Not a bug. It's a slug.
Slowly gliding by on its trail of slime.

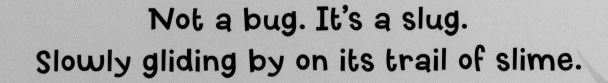

Let's just wait for it to leave.

Slugs *slide.*

But not very fast.

Time to be patient.

Finally, it's just about gone.

That sure took a while.

**Hey,** a couple of pillbugs! This will be fun.

Let's give them a light ta*p* and watch them cur*l* up into little balls.

Then *tip up* the bottom of the book so they roll into the grass.

# Wheeee!

No wonder they're also called roly-polies.

## Pillbugs curl!

Lay the book back down.

**Plop!** lands a treefrog.

Lift up the book and flip it over
so the pages face the ground.
Will the frog drop off?

# Nope!

## Treefrogs stick.

And it looks like this one is stuck tight.

Lay the book back down.

Here come some ants!

Lots of them!

Maybe they will leave on their own.

Or maybe not.

Use your hand to guide them
off the top of the page.

Off goes the army of ants.

Ants *march.*

# Yikes!
The frog is still here.

Good-bye, ant.

**Oh, no!** The snake is back.

Is it hungry, too?

Good-bye, frog.

Good-bye, snake.

Hello, beetle! You're back!

You won't believe who
was just here.

# Let's Move Along

When you or I want to go somewhere, we can move in many different ways. We can walk. We can hop. We can skip. When we're in danger, we usually run — very fast! Some animals also walk and run. But many move in other ways, too.

**Beetles** usually crawl. But when they need to move quickly to escape from danger, they fly. Their outer shell is made of two hard wings. Underneath those wings are two more delicate wings. When it's time to fly, they lift the two hard upper wings out of the way. Then they spread their other wings and lift into the air. The beetle in this book is a *Grapevine Beetle*.

**Snakes** do not have legs or wings to carry them away. They expand and contract their muscles to move like a wave. Scales on their belly grab the ground so they can push forward. Some are even able to climb up trees. Snakes are very flexible. They can coil and wrap their body around things to hold on tightly. The snake in this book is a *Ribbon Snake*.

**Grasshoppers** usually crawl and climb slowly. But when they need to get to safety in a hurry, they hop. They use their powerful back legs to launch themselves into the air. Sometimes they

open their wings and fly. But most of the time they just land where their hop takes them. The grasshopper in this book is a *Lubber Grasshopper*.

**Spiders** have special glands to make silk. They use their silk to make webs and catch prey. If a spider falls from its web, it can hang from a silk thread and pull itself back up. Young spiders are called spiderlings. Sometimes they hang on a thread of silk and let the wind carry them to a new place. The spider in this book is a *Marbled Orb Weaver*.

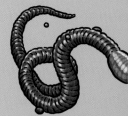

**Earthworms** move like snakes by expanding and contracting their muscles. But instead of scales, they have tiny bristles to help them push through the soil. It's dangerous for a worm to be above ground because many animals will try to eat it! When it feels threatened, a worm wriggles back and forth. This makes it harder for an animal to grab to it. The worm in this book is a *Nightcrawler*. It's also called a *Common Earthworm*.

**Slugs** move very slowly. They make slime and slide along on one foot. You can see where slugs have been by the slime trails they leave behind. Slugs don't have many ways to defend themselves. Luckily, most animals don't like to eat them. They're too gooey! The slug in this book is a *Leopard Slug*.

**Pillbugs** aren't bugs. They're more like shrimp and crabs. They have 14 legs to carry them around. They live beneath rocks and logs where the soil stays damp. They curl up in a tight ball to keep from drying out. They also roll into a ball to protect their soft underbelly. Armadillos do this, too. Pillbugs are also known as *Roly-Polies* or *Armadillo Bugs*.

**Treefrogs** are a kind of frog. They spend most of their time in shrubs and trees. They have pads on their toes. These "toe pads" make their fingers look like little lollipops. The mucous on their toe pads is sticky. It's sticky enough to help them grab onto a surface. But not so sticky that they get stuck there forever. The frog in this book is a *Gray Treefrog*.

**Ants**, like all insects, have six legs. How can they move six legs at one time? Ants have it figured out. Every time they take a step, they move the front leg and the back leg on one side and the middle leg on the other side. If they need to go faster, they take longer steps. No matter how fast they march, they never tip over because they always have one or two legs on each side touching the ground. The ants in this book are *Carpenter Ants*.

## What You See is What You Get

All of the animals in this book are close to their actual sizes. They're commonly found in the U.S. and Canada. Look for them in your own backyard or nearby park.

## What's a Bug?

In everyday language, an insect is a bug. Insects do not have a backbone. Instead, they have a hard outer shell. Their body is made up of three parts—a head, thorax, and abdomen. All insects have six legs and two antennae. Almost all insects also have wings.

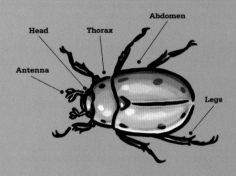

## How Many Legs?

Is a spider an insect? To help you decide, count the legs. Does it have six legs? *No, it has eight legs.* Then it's not an insect. It belongs to group of animals called arachnids [uh-RACK-nidz]. In this book there are three insects. Can you find them? Count their legs.

# Insects and More

As children learned on the previous page, an insect has certain characteristics—a hard outer shell, three body parts, six legs, two antennae, and usually wings. The three insects presented in this book are the beetle, grasshopper, and ant. Other critters in the book that aren't insects—but that are often called bugs—are the spider, pillbug, and even the worm and slug. However, there are two animals in this book that are definitely not bugs—the snake and the frog.

## Activity: Moving Along

Children interact with this book to discover that some animals fly, while others hop, coil, hang, slide, curl, stick, and march. Read and discuss the information in "Move It Along" on the previous pages. Then show the free, online video "How Animals Move" available at www.thebugchicks.com. It's about three minutes long and appropriate for children of all ages. Have children notice what animals in the book are also in the video. Ask them what movements are included in the video but not in the book. This and other entertaining bug-related videos are produced by The Bug Chicks, entomologists Kristie Reddick and Jessica Honaker.

# Movement is a Matter of Survival

The animals in the book moved when they felt threatened. Each used its body in a different way to escape danger and survive. Read the information about how animals move on the previous "Explore More for Kids" pages. Then reinforce the concepts by playing this movement game.

## Activity: Escape Like A...

Establish a boundary for the game called the "safe zone." Choose one child to be the "Critter Catcher," and have that person stand in the center of the playing area. Everyone else sits on the floor or ground. The distance between the Critter Catcher and the rest of the group will depend on the age of the children playing. The object of the game is to escape the Critter Catcher by moving like the animal the Critter Catcher calls out. For example, if the Critter Catcher calls out "Snake," everyone on the floor puts their hands to their sides and slithers away like a snake. The Critter Catcher tries to tag the snakes before they make it to the safe zone. Once tagged, the snake must stop moving. The snake must also stop moving if it bumps into another snake. The first snake that gets to the safety zone becomes the next Critter Catcher. The play continues with all nine animals in the book.

# Do You See What I See?

Scientists are skilled in observation and recording what they see. In these activities, children practice their observation skills. Magnifying glasses or hand lenses help kids get a closer look at the critters they find.

## Activity: Take a Closer Look

Select a section of grassy area (part of a yard, lawn, or playground). Push four sharpened pencils into the soil in a one-foot square pattern. Tie string around the pencils, making a miniature "boxing ring" on the ground. You may want to create several rings, depending on the size of your class.

Have children get on their hands and knees and look closely inside the square. If they look carefully enough and long enough they'll begin to see many different critters. You may want to have them keep some "Field Notes" of the different types of animals they see inside the ring using words and/or sketches. Have children note the movements, habits, or behaviors of any animals (ants, grasshoppers, caterpillars, worms) as they travel (jump, crawl, slither) through the ring. You might want to have them visit their "rings" frequently over a period of several weeks. (This activity is by Tony Fredericks and is based on his book *Under One Rock*, https://dawnpub.com/activity/rock/)

## Activity: Create a Mini-Beast Hotel

Show children how to invite a variety of creatures to your backyard or school playground by creating a mini-beast hotel. Your hotel can be as simple as a wooden board placed on the ground. Or just turn a clay pot upside down under a bush. Wait a couple of days and then look underneath it. Insects and other critters that like a cool, dark, moist environment may have moved in. Look carefully for roly-polies, ants, beetles, and others. Hotels can be created out of various manmade and natural items. Amphibians might be attracted to a pile of stones, old roof tiles, or bricks. Some insects would find pinecones, dry leaves, and bits of bark inviting.

## Engineering an Insect

Observing how insects move and maneuver over obstacles has inspired engineers to create robots that perform all kinds of tasks, from search and rescue operations to exploring the environment. The following activity doesn't have your children building robots, but it does have them engineering a make-believe insect of their own.

## Activity: Design an Insect

Review the characteristics of an insect with your children, and have them design an insect that has at least one moving part. Ask them to explain how their insect moves and eats and where it lives. Then have children make a model of their insect using materials you provide (towel holders, plastic and paper cups, straws, pipe cleaners, foam balls, construction paper, and various other objects). Allow time for children to test out their models, evaluate how they moved, and make changes. Be sure to debrief the results of their experimentation.

Scan the QR Code and scroll to "Activities" to access more activities, educational resources, and standards-based lesson plans.

**JOHN HIMMELMAN IS A NATURALIST** and author/illustrator of many books for children and adults. His curiosity about all things wild has led him to many interesting places in the world. His favorite place to enjoy nature, though, is in his own Connecticut backyard. He rarely leaves his little overgrown meadow without having found something new and exciting. He is married to Betsy, who is also an artist and naturalist.

Visit his website at www.johnhimmelman.com.

## MORE DAWN BOOKS BY JOHN HIMMELMAN

*Noisy Bug Sing-Along*—Bugs can be very LOUD! And they have no "voices," but instead rub legs or wings together, or use other body parts to make sounds. Fascinating! Available as a book app—each page is animated, plus there is an interactive game at the end.

*Noisy Frog Sing-Along*—Frogs make all kinds of weird and wonderful sounds—all without ever opening their mouths! Enjoy John's great close-up illustrations and croak! Available as a book app—each page is animated, plus there is an interactive game at the end.

*Noisy Bird Sing-Along*—Every kind of bird has its very own kind of sound! Cheerful sounds, mournful sounds, sweet sounds, weird sounds. You can tell who they are without even opening your eyes. And what fun to sing along.

## MORE DAWN BOOKS ABOUT CRITTERS

*Under One Rock*—A whole community of creatures lives under rocks. No child will be able to resist taking a peek after reading this book.

*In the Trees, Honeybees!*—Remarkable inside-the-hive views of bees offer insights into the lives of these important insects.

*The Prairie that Nature Built*—Meet the multitude of species that live on the prairie as you take a trip above, below, and all around this beautiful and exciting habitat.

*Wild Ones: Observing City Critters*—Follow the curious and adorable dog Scooter as he travels through an urban landscape, seeing many wild animals, and not seeing many others.

Dawn Publications is dedicated to inspiring in children a deeper understanding and appreciation for all life on Earth. You can browse through our titles, download resources for teachers, and order at www.dawnpub.com or call 800-545-7475.